# TIMELESS
## PRINCIPLES OF
# INVESTING
## (IN REAL ESTATE)

# TIMELESS PRINCIPLES OF INVESTING (IN REAL ESTATE)

## The Keys to Building Real Wealth And Keeping It!

FUQUAN BILAL

Printed in the United States of America.
First paperback edition June 2022.

Cover design by Mocah Studio, LLC
Layout design by G Sharp Design, LLC.

ISBN 979-8-9864816-3-0

# Contents

# Preface

**There are proven timeless principles** for investing, and specifically for succeeding at investing in real estate. Following them makes intelligent financial decisions far simpler and enables investors to avoid the common blunders that end up burning so many others.

There is so much potential out there. There is so much opportunity. Yet riding the latest fads, defaulting to letting the wrong money managers make all the decisions, and forgetting these timeless principles robs so many of the security, prosperity, lives, and impact they could easily have. It is also tragic to see so many following poor advice and momentary celebrities only to end up crashing and burning and losing everything they thought they made.

For more than two decades, I've witnessed how using these principles creates financial success or ignoring them causes the loss of it.

I'll have to admit that I may not have always gotten these principles right myself, especially when I started out in business and investing in real estate. There are many misconceptions about these principles and what they really mean. However, I've practiced them, studied them, and followed their history back hundreds and thousands of years to see how they've worked, as well as how even the seemingly most successful wealthy individuals and organizations have been taken down by diverting from them.

These principles have created the greatest wealth in history — individual wealth in the tens of billions of dollars — or have made companies worth tens of billions of dollars evaporate almost overnight.

In this book, I bring together these ageless guides to investing that will help you get on the right track and see real results faster while ensuring you'll get to keep the benefit of those results. I dig into their real meaning and best applications. I reveal the nuances that often trick investors, and how to use them well.

Whether you are brand-new to investing and perhaps still in school, or you are an experienced investor with a sizable portfolio, this book will give you new insights. It will become your best ally in making financial decisions and ensuring that your success lasts.

This book belongs on every investor's shelf and in every family's home. As it proves its value to you, I am sure you will want to keep it there for generations and share it with those you care about.

Whatever you aspire to, or want to avoid, let these timeless principles be your guide.

# Introduction

**The Timeless Principles** of Investing in Real Estate are your allies and guides to getting what is most important to you while avoiding common — and expensive — detours and mistakes.

Investing is often made to seem either complicated and intimidating or sometimes too simplistic. This often stunts the potential you have in life and robs you of what could be.

In this book, you will find clear guiding principles that will steer your investment choices in the right direction. You will find crisp and easy-to-understand principles to set yourself in the right direction as a new investor, as well as the depth you need as a more experienced real estate pro to cut through the misconceptions and keep excelling where others see it all fall apart. I provide new insights that you may not have thought of, and certainly won't find even in some of those $40,000 real estate investing courses.

These are not fad rules that trap investors in rough rules of thumb or calculations that end up doing more harm than good and don't apply in all phases of the market. Rather, these are truly immutable and enduring principles that the investors you admire most have used to build and retain their own wealth and credit their success with.

Whenever you see true success at work out there, these principles will be the foundation behind it. And when you see huge fails, they can be directly traced back to breaking them.

They've been proven for hundreds and thousands of years. Those that are not truly eternal have been stripped out.

This book does not sell any particular investment or strategy. It is an unbiased guide to finding the best way for you to master your financial game, for both swift and lasting success, with modern applications. Use it to be sure you are heading in the right direction and to make safer, more intelligent investments.

The principles in this book will help streamline your decision-making, give you more confidence, and ensure you don't end up broke.

## Chapter 1

# TIMELESS PRINCIPLE #1: DIVERSIFY, DIVERSIFY, DIVERSIFY

*"Divide your investments among many places, for you do not know what risks might lie ahead."*—King Solomon

**We've all heard** the saying "Don't put all your eggs in one basket." The principle of diversification is far deeper and more important than that.

In fact, this principle is so important that I dedicated a whole book just to it (see Book 1 in this series, *The Guide to Diversifying in Real Estate for the Intelligent Real Estate Investor*). I believe even experienced, veteran investors will be challenged by it and find new ways to consider and build smarter and more meaningful diversification into their investing.

This principle dates back at least 3,000 years and to some of the earliest human writings. It was one of the key principles the wise King Solomon used to build a net worth estimated to be around $2.2T today, as well as around $40B in passive income per year[1] — figures that blow away today's greats by a long, long way.

Unfortunately, diversification is also one of the most misunderstood investment principles. Here are some of the key points that we all need to know and remember.

# YOUR HOME IS NOT AN INVESTMENT PROPERTY

One of the big myths and pitfalls is that your home residence qualifies as a part of your investments. *It doesn't.*

This mistake leads many to end up severely underexposed to real estate in their finances and investment portfolio. That can be an expensive mistake.

Yes, you may feel like buying a home, and a second and third is a form of investment. Structured well, in the right entity, with the right leverage, in the right location, where you have strong legal homestead protections and low transfer taxes, it can be beneficial. It can be smart. Just don't confuse this with your investment *portfolio.*

As long as you are alive, or your family or heirs are using it, your home is *not* a true investment. You'll always be using it as a roof over your head, and it might appreciate in value against the time when

---

1 https://www.marketwatch.com/story/richest-men-in-history-vladimir-puti n-bill-gates-and-warren-buffett-arent-even-close-2017-08-09#:~:text=Then%20 there's%20King%20Solomon%2C%20who,his%20fortune%20to%20%242.2%20trillion.

you're ready to sell the property. But it isn't liquid, or delivering passive income every month. If you end up refinancing to tap any equity appreciation, then you often take on bad debt that has to be repaid with earned income versus pure investment properties.

Your home residence is not counted as a part of your net worth. That should be a big tell of its own.

If you have been mis-categorizing the role of your home in your investment strategy so far, take this moment to recalibrate your financial plan to account for it, and make sure you are invested appropriately in the real estate sector with the rest of your portfolio. You may need to make a big shift in your asset allocation to make up for this, and quickly.

# DON'T PUT ALL YOUR EGGS IN ONE BASKET

This is an important principle as well. Unfortunately, many stop right here with this sentence when it comes to understanding their need to diversify. Their next move is simply to diversify — just for the sake of it.

Traditional or antiquated brokerages often feed this issue, putting their clients' money into all types of baskets without really delivering true diversification or helping clients achieve better financial objectives.

Whether it is for a retirement plan, diversifying from holding cash in the bank, or trying to get ahead by investing directly in real estate, avoid putting everything into one basket. That is just gambling. The house always wins.

As far back as 450 BC (over 2,470 years ago), King Solomon reportedly wrote, "Invest in seven ventures, yes, in eight; you do not know what disaster may come upon the land." Also translated as, "But divide your investments among many places, for you do not know what risks might lie ahead." It seemed to work out well for him, and it's probably not a bad starting point for your own portfolio diversification.

# POOR DIVERSIFICATION CAN BE JUST AS BAD AS NONE

What many don't fully appreciate is how dangerous poor diversification can be as well.

Blind and careless diversification is almost as risky as not diversifying at all.

Sadly, this is where most end up by default. It is where you are now if you have abdicated your financial decisions and future to an old-school broker or 401k plan.

Putting your eggs in different baskets doesn't help if they are all held by the same hand, have the same handle, are in the same henhouse, or have holes in them.

Most people who rely on brokers don't know what they are invested in, why, how it works, or who is making the decisions. They are told they are diversified widely and get warm and fuzzy feelings from it. They think they can sleep at night.

If you read *The Guide to Diversifying in Real Estate for the Intelligent Real Estate Investor*, you will gain a whole new perspective on diversification; its true purpose; and what real, wise diversification looks like.

Lacking good diversification, you will almost inevitably find all your investments failing simultaneously, typically right at the worst moment — when you need them to be delivering or available.

# TYPES OF DIVERSIFICATION

Here is a quick overview of the elements of real and comprehensive diversification, and what it should be doing for you. You can aim for:

- Geographic diversification
- Volume diversification
- Depth of diversification

**Asset diversification** may include:

- Single-family homes
- Multi-family properties
- Commercial properties
- Tax liens
- Performing mortgage notes
- Nonperforming loans (NPLs)

**Diversified strategies** may include:

- Value-add investing (fix and flip, repositioning, etc.)
- Opportunistic investments
- Passive income-producing investments

### What a *correctly* diversified investment portfolio can do for you:

- Simultaneously achieve multiple objectives
- Future-proof your finances
- Create concrete downside protection for wealth preservation
- Provide above-average returns
- Yield passive income
- Provide consistent results and predictability in planning
- Grow wealth
- Satisfy short-, medium-, and long-term needs and goals

# THE ROLES OF DIFFERENT INVESTMENTS IN YOUR FINANCES AND LIFE

Here are some examples of the roles that types of investments can play in your finances and life:

- Performing mortgage notes: predictable cash flow and yields
- Nonperforming mortgage notes: wealth gains and higher yields
- Second mortgages: higher yields
- Private lending: high yields and security
- Fund investments: passive income and ROI on time
- Fixing and flipping properties: lump-sum gains and leaps in wealth
- Rental properties: passive income and tax advantages

Before executing your new financial plan and funding a new round of investments, make sure you have a full appreciation of the need and value of full breadth and depth of diversification.

## Chapter 2

# TIMELESS PRINCIPLE #2: DON'T LOSE MONEY

*"Rule Number 1: Don't lose money. Rule Number 2: Never forget rule number one."—Warren Buffett*

**It sounds obvious,** right? Yet if you look at the investments and financial choices of most people and organizations, you wouldn't think they ever heard of this principle.

Of course, the unexpected always happens, anything that can go wrong will eventually, even the best-laid plans get wrinkles in them. But that doesn't mean you shouldn't be positive. Plenty of ways exist to mitigate these factors, which is why diversification is such an important principle.

Still, to take advantage of the best opportunities and keep growing, you may have some losses. Providing you always make far more than you lose, though, that is irrelevant. In fact, you could argue it is better to lose $10,000 if it means you make an extra $1M each year.

Still, the point is that not losing money should be pretty high up there on your list of criteria when evaluating investment options.

# WHAT IT MEANS

This is so important because if you lose money, you don't have any capital to reinvest. You are back to zero. Even if you don't gain, if you don't lose, you will survive to fight to win another day.

Of course, being too conservative is financially deadly, too. You have to be constantly improving, although you don't want to lose.

It may be getting old, but I've said several times that investors have to prioritize Return of Investment as their primary ROI evaluation, over Return on Investment. Sadly, some financial firms use this as an excuse to deliver subpar results and negligible returns to their investors. You don't have to settle for that, either.

# WHEN YOU DO LOSE MONEY

If you do lose money, don't lose heart. Even the best-looking investment opportunities can end up losing money and becoming disasters with poor management, if risks haven't been foreseen and planned for.

Take a moment to compartmentalize and learn from the experience. Then move forward.

Was this a planned and accounted-for loss? Part of regularly doing business and within the range of risk previously assessed and forecast?

If so, you are probably on the right track.

If not, what went right? What went wrong?

More importantly, what can be done better to mitigate and insulate you from this risk in the future?

Make adjustments to your management or portfolio and keep pressing forward. These moments can often relegate you to a decade or more of misery and mediocrity, or propel and launch you to better things and results while protecting you the next time a similar scenario arises.

You have 90% of this within your control. It's how you react and get proactive and choose to view things that matters most.

# IDLE CAPITAL IS LOSING MONEY

As mentioned, being overly cautious and conservative can be counterproductive. In fact, this is often the real source of loss that individuals, funds, and investors experience.

It is smart to have some cash on hand, as well as some emergency funds with low penalties for withdrawal in a crunch. Three, six, or 12 months of cash to cover basic essentials and outstanding debt service is typically sufficient. Exactly how much you need and is smart can fluctuate based on external factors like the economy and risk levels, as well as job security, health, etc.

Having too much in these types of cash investments can be self-sabotaging. This is because they usually offer zero to minimal returns — often net negative returns, once you do the real math on taxes, fees, and inflation. This money is normally devaluing.

COVID-19 is a great example of this. With real inflation at the store and pump often reaching 30% in the year after COVID-related restrictions began, your cash on hand was effectively worth 30% less. If you had $10,000 in the bank at the start, it would only buy you $7,000 worth of things. With the same pace of inflation the following year, that same $10,000 would only buy you $4,900 worth of the same products, and so on. It's a race to zero, and time is working against you.

Even if you aren't hitting your target returns on every deal, clearly putting that money to work makes it less likely you'll be losing money. It will at least minimize and soften those losses (unless you are really terrible at evaluating, selecting, and managing investments).

To ensure your target or expected returns will keep you ahead, make sure you do the full math before you invest — but do keep up your momentum.

Remember that any idle capital will eat away at any positive returns you make elsewhere.

Fortune favors those who take action.

# HOW TO AVOID LOSING MONEY

With the main point here being not to lose money, how can you avoid it — both individual investment losses and net losses?

## Over-Collateralized Investments

Over-collateralizing investments is a good start. For example, buying at discounts and below value, such as buying mortgage loan notes for less than the unpaid principal balance, or picking up REOs or tax liens to secure physical real estate assets for less than they will sell for on the open market.

If you can generate returns, cash flow, or other profits from these investments while you hold them, that is great and can help you avoid losses. Even if you have to sell at a discount from market value, you should still be able to make a great profit.

Investing in select real estate funds is another way to do this. If you put in $100,000 and the fund holds $5M in real estate assets, there is tangible value that is far greater than the investment you made, even if some of those assets underperform.

Other types of financial leverage can achieve this by sharing your risk with a lender and their investors, which minimizes your exposure.

## Hard Assets for Downside Protection

If you've invested in startups, publicly traded stocks, or cryptocurrency before, you know that your investment can go to zero fast, often virtually overnight. When that happens, you can have nothing to bounce back with or to regrow with. In contrast, if you have hard assets, you can't lose everything, even if temporary paper value fluctuations occur. You can always bounce back.

The great news is these can still be strong performing investments, with cash flow and above-average total returns. You don't have to sacrifice one for the other.

Be cautious with funds of funds of funds, or publicly traded stocks, even in the real estate and debt sector, that don't really cover your money with hard assets, or where so much debt overshadows your capital that investors will be left high and dry in a crunch.

## Asset Allocation

Asset allocation is also a big part of avoiding net losses. Paper gains and losses are always fluctuating. They don't mean real losses unless you sell and cash out of an investment. Still, you never want to be too far down at any one time. You can't afford everything to be down at the same time. You have to be pushing growth, while not betting everything on one horse.

This is where diversification comes in. And intelligent diversification is more than just the volume of units in your portfolio or where they are.

This is where you can allocate a percentage of your portfolio to investments less likely to lose value or face extinction, along with others that aggressively push growth and ought to deliver high enough returns to offset any temporary losses you do have on overly conservative investments, along with income investments that can keep delivering in the middle.

The optimal percentage allocations in these different categories will vary based on several factors, including:

1. Age and time before you retire
2. Expectations of returns
3. Timing of the market, and how bearish or bullish you are
4. Risk tolerance

## Chapter 3

# TIMELESS PRINCIPLE #3: EXPECT VOLATILITY AND PROFIT FROM IT

*"Volatility is your friend as an investor, if you know how to use it."—Fuquan Bilal*

**Even the seemingly** most stable places to park your money have volatility. Even cash in your mattress, a savings account, and gold fluctuate in value.

Failing to anticipate volatility or being shocked when it happens doesn't feel great, but volatility doesn't have to be bad. It can be your best ally. It can provide some of the greatest leaps in your wealth that you couldn't otherwise achieve in several lifetimes. In fact, you might say that those at the very top of the game purposely create volatility specifically to create gains that are otherwise impossible. Of course, volatility cuts both ways. Failing to appreciate it, or using it as a tool, is like a double-edged knife that is blunt on the front side, but easily slashes your own finances on the back side.

There are three things to respect about volatility:

1. Volatility is inevitable.
2. Volatility is not a risk, but an opportunity.
3. You can profit from volatility.

# CHANGE IS INEVITABLE AND CONSTANT

One of the most powerful lessons we can learn in life is that change is inevitable. The earlier we can learn this in life, the easier life goes. It is when we don't that things are extra-hard.

There is a popular saying that the only guarantees in life are death and taxes. I think some might argue that those aren't absolutes anymore. Some people cheat on their taxes, and plenty of scientific efforts are being made to prolong life, or even freeze people or upload them to the cloud. Perhaps the only single thing we can count on in life is that everything will change. Nothing stays the same forever.

We don't stay the same age. The economy doesn't stay the same. Our cars don't last forever. Presidents, government administrations, and their policies and direction are replaced. The landscape and skyline are always evolving. What's trending online changes by the minute. Individual market sectors and asset values are in flux.

Some of these changes are clearly moving far more slowly than others, while some can be extremely rapid. You may not get a single gray hair for 40 years. A tree may take 20 years to grow to a point where it makes sense to harvest it. Real estate may go up at an average of 5% per year over the long run. Some public stock investors have seen their portfolios plunge by 70% overnight. As Warren Buffett has said, "Unless you can watch your stockholding decline by 50% without becoming panic-stricken, you should not be in the stock market."

Simply put, volatility is the one thing you can bank on.

# VOLATILITY IS NOT RISK, BUT OPPORTUNITY

The only real risk of volatility is failing to recognize that it is happening. Failing to foresee it causes a lot of pain, heartache, and stress. That's true from being a kid and seeing your childhood friends move away, to growing up and realizing your parents are aging, to both thinking your tough financial situation is permanent or failing to protect yourself when you think you've got it made.

Volatility isn't only something you shouldn't be fearful of, it is something you should embrace. After all, without volatility, there are no gains. The more volatility there is, often the more opportunity there is. If asset values don't go up at all, we'd lose money across the board. If they never went down, there wouldn't be dips to buy in.

There are three great ways to profit from volatility as an investor:

1. Organic appreciation and gains as things go up
2. Discounts and better value buys when prices are down
3. Creating volatility

## Organic Appreciation

One of the easiest ways to profit from volatility is to simply hold onto assets. Over the long term, real estate has mostly gone up in value.

According to the Federal Reserve Bank in St. Louis,[2] the median home sales price in the U.S. in 1963 was just $17,800. By 2021, that had reached $404,700. That is almost half a million dollars in organic gains per property you bought and held over that time. Just 13 of those would be enough to enable the average individual investor and family to retire pretty well.

If this is a rental property, ideally you are also banking passive income from these assets every month during this time. Even clearing $1,000 a month from each unit is $12,000 a year per unit in passive income just from these investments. Not a huge sum on its own, but a pretty healthy level of additional spending money each month, especially with a nest egg worth over $5M.

Of course, most of the greatest leaps in wealth come during times of distress and when volatility has driven down pricing. This is when you can pick up assets for pennies on the dollar more easily.

We'll get into volatility even more, and how to profit from it, as we cover the principle of not following the herd, along with some examples of how others have done it and made fortunes worth billions of dollars in the process.

## Creating Volatility and Value

Creating volatility is a controversial subject. It is often mired in sketchiness. Yet it is what those at the very top of the financial game are all about. Billions are spent on faster internet connections and owning publications, new websites, and analytics sites to sway the markets.

This can get murky and contentious when you start talking about the biggest financial institutions manipulating the housing market

---

2    https://fred.stlouisfed.org/series/MSPUS.

to seize millions of homes, and then resell them for profit and issue new loans on them at higher rates and for more origination fees. Gentrification and allowing communities to become crime-ridden and depressed are often other forms of forced volatility.

For the most part, it is best to steer clear of these methods to avoid even dancing in those gray areas of ethical mud and legal liability. However, one of the powerful things about the real estate sector in particular is the ability to push positive volatility by adding value responsibly and cleanly.

Such control over the value of your own assets, portfolio, and financial future is almost unique to this sector.

There are many ways to do this, including:

- Rehabbing and renovating buildings
- Repositioning, repurposing, and remarketing properties
- Improving marketability of assets by clearing liens and title clouds
- Improving performance through smarter leasing, increasing rents, and optimizing management efficiency and cost effectiveness
- Making improvements to land, such as building new construction
- Repackaging mortgage loan notes
- Creating re-performing notes from nonperforming notes
- Increasing access to assets that others don't have

It's also worth noting that interim volatility is frequently meaningless, or inconsequential. Paper losses aren't real losses, at least not until an asset is liquidated, although they can affect you mentally, as well as your perceived financial strength and power, especially if you are not mentally tough. You sometimes need a strong stomach to see the big picture rather than focusing on today's ticker feed.

## Buying Low

Here is how some others see volatility when it comes to investing.

"A smart investor is excited about the returns one gets from a bull market, and super-excited about low-cost investment one makes in a bear market. It's a win-win both ways! Volatility is an investor's best friend!"—Manoj Arora

"The first rule of investment is 'buy low and sell high,' but many people fear to buy low because of the fear of the stock dropping even lower. Then you may ask: 'When is the time to buy low?' The answer is: When there is maximum pessimism."—Sir John Templeton

"Basically, price fluctuations have only one significant meaning for the true investor. They provide . . . an opportunity to buy wisely when prices fall sharply and to sell wisely when they advance a great deal."—Benjamin Graham

You see, the downslope of volatility is also incredibly profitable. It provides a moment when you can buy mortgage notes for 40 cents on the dollar or properties for as little as 30 cents on the dollar — sometimes even less, especially when using mortgage notes or tax liens as a back door to gain access to this inventory. The deeper the distress and the lower things drop, the better the upside can be.

Don't be afraid to buy when things slide or seem at rock bottom. You know that change is inevitable, and they won't stay there forever.

# ARE YOU AN INVESTOR OR A SPECTATOR?

There are two ways to engage with volatility. One is as a speculator. The other is as an investor.

Speculating is just another word for gambling and makes people feel like they are making a smarter decision; one they see as more intelligent than just putting the same amount of money into scratch-off cards, lottery tickets, or playing roulette in Las Vegas. In reality, purely speculative investing may be even riskier, with lower odds of winning than going to the casino or playing scratch-offs.

This is most notable because speculators are often last into the market, when it is inevitably going to go down, and the data experts have already shown the bubble has popped. They are grabbing the hot potato right when everyone else quits the game, which leaves them burned.

Appreciation is great. If you get appreciation, and especially organic wealth increases on your investments in addition to the value-add plays you make and the income that investment already produces, that is a nice bonus. However, it should never be the only reason or basis for putting money into something.

Only a few appear to win from speculation. Either they are simply lucky, or they are manipulating the market and controlling values, sucking in all the money from speculators before creating a "correction."

On the other hand, *true investors* are basing their decisions on the existing value of investments and their performance; ability to add value and enhance performance of undervalued and underperforming assets; and ability to use advanced, deep knowledge and discipline to take advantage of and profit from volatility.

## Chapter 4

# TIMELESS PRINCIPLE # 4: DON'T BE FOOLED INTO THINKING YOU CAN TIME THE MARKET PERFECTLY

**One of the most financially** deadly mistakes that amateur investors make is believing they can time the market.

It is true that there are normally relatively predictable cycles in the economy, individual industries, and the real estate markets. A lot of profit can be made by understanding and working these cycles. But it is not about drinking your own Kool-Aid to the point of delirium.

Rather, the upper hand and winnings go to those who respect the fact that they don't own completely accurate crystal balls.

Aristotle said, "Knowing yourself is the beginning of all wisdom." John Maxwell puts it as, "To grow yourself, you must know yourself." This is certainly true when it comes to your money and investing. You have to be wary of your own ego. Know your strengths, and own your weaknesses and limitations.

# TIMING THE MARKETS AND WILD CARDS

As we've already covered, nothing ever stays the same; volatility is virtually guaranteed. Looking at history, some predictable cycles have occurred. We've often seen economies and markets rotate every seven to 15 years. Overall, it has been almost like clockwork for a very long time. These cycles can be tracked back internationally for thousands of years.

There are some very clear indicators of these rotations and phases of the market, too. The four main phases are:

1. Recovery
2. Expansion
3. Hyper-supply
4. Recession

These phases play out on the smallest local levels, and at macro global levels as well; a feature that has become more common and influential the more global and intertwined international economies and markets have become. If you want to think really big, you might even consider some of our most ancient civilizations, like the Mayans, Egypt, and Rome.

There are lots of indicators and metrics to track to maintain some insights on when these turns are coming, including affordability, supply, interest rates and underwriting standards, liquidity, and consumer sentiment. Most of it is really common sense. Yet that is often sidelined in favor of flawed metrics and claims in the media.

Experienced investors know there are also plenty of wild cards that can disrupt and alter these cycles. They can shorten or extend them, although there is little proof that anyone or any government has figured out how to completely mitigate them, even if they wanted to. These include natural disasters — hurricanes, earthquakes, wildfires, and tsunamis can all affect cycles, as can acts of war. At least on a local level, they can compound the impacts of these market turns.

This can go both ways. As we perhaps saw most visibly in the wake of the COVID-19 pandemic, there can be stimuli, government intervention, and artificial manipulation of markets.

Stimuli can be injected to cover up for weakness, and may artificially extend positive runs, at least for a while. Markets can be artificially manipulated to appear as if there is a shortage of assets, such as real estate owned (REO) and retail homes for sale, in turn jacking up prices and bidding wars on the retail consumer side of the market.

At other moments, crashes, recessions, and depressions seem to be caused by policies, or at least compounded by them, such as raising interest rates and cutting access to credit. It isn't always clear whether these are foolish decisions due to lessons from previous cycles not being learned, or cards played intentionally to force a "correction."

Know your cycles and the factors that drive them. Also understand that other factors you cannot always precisely calculate and time will occur.

Now let's look at some of the most common ways investors are fooled or fool themselves here.

# FORECASTS AND PREDICTIONS

Some have said that there are only two people who can be wrong every time, all the time, and still keep their jobs and get paid: weather forecasters and Realtors.

In some places, if they say it will rain, you can safely plan your outdoor event, because it definitely won't. If they say it will be clear with zero chance of rain, you can bet that rain will fall. The same often seems true of stock market analysts and economists.

Many Realtors also have the habit of always saying it is time to buy and sell — at the same time. While this may be true for investors, it rarely is for retail home buyers. Even the National Association of Realtors has previously gone back and restated years of data, well after the fact.

Expert insights are important in every area of life, especially when it comes to our money. Yet this information has to be weighed against an understanding of the motivations, views, and agendas of whoever is providing those insights. Not everyone who claims to be an expert really is one.

Again, don't forget your common sense.

Fundamentals and data you don't see may exist. Not everyone has access to the behind-the-scenes data or minds of those sitting on inventory. However, issues can be pretty easy to spot if you are tuned into the market. Even listening to what other consumers are saying at the gym, coffee shop, and local restaurants will reveal a lot about consumer sentiment and trends.

The bottom line here is that with the right information, we can get a good feel for where the market currently is and is going, although even the most established pros and organizations frequently fail miserably at calling the precise timing of the market. Just look at Zillow, which, after plowing many billions into its efforts, ended up admitting defeat and had to lay off at least 25% of its workforce and close down its main business, citing their inability to forecast property prices.

# EGO AND THE MIDAS TOUCH

One of the biggest and most tragic traps for real estate investors and business owners is falling for the belief that they have the Midas touch. They may achieve a lot of perceived success in a very short period of time, often in easy bull runs, when it is virtually impossible for anyone to lose money. Many get in and quickly start making millions, build a portfolio of millions of dollars of property, or even have their businesses valued at tens of billions of dollars.

They think it is all them, they are geniuses, and nothing they do will go wrong. This is when they start slacking off, stop learning, and throw caution and common sense out the window.

This ego-driven behavior directly affects the ability to time the market and act accordingly.

Note that in contrast, the truly successful investors over the long haul are typically the humblest, and openly admit they are terrible at timing the market themselves. Success is not about perfect timing. It is far more about understanding this handicap.

# "IT'S DIFFERENT THIS TIME"

These are the famous last words that inevitably lead to serious financial losses.

This can apply to both recovery and recessionary periods of the market. Some believe the market will magically go up forever just because it has for a couple of years, or that there is no bottom, because prices have come down substantially.

At least up to now, since the beginning of human history, it hasn't been different. Of course, this could absolutely be one of the times I'll have to admit I'm wrong, and specifically about market timing, but it seems very unlikely.

When you hear "it's different this time," take it as a huge red flag. That's your warning sign to take action, because others have been drinking way too much Kool-Aid.

# "WE'VE GOT ANOTHER 12 TO 18 MONTHS"

You'll probably hear this claim not too long after "it's different this time."

The problem here is this is often repeated again and again, for 12, 18, or 24 months, and typically without any change in strategy or preparation. Guess what? All of a sudden, it has been far more than 18 months, the market has already changed, and it is too late to adjust and escape the consequences.

Once a downturn shows up in public data, it has already been happening for months because it takes time to compile and report data. It may have been going on for three, six, 12 months or more by the time data is compiled and released, and the media picks up on it.

If you think you've got another 12 to 18 months to take advantage of market trends, adjust for it now. Minimize your exposure to loss and being stuck, while finding sound ways to participate in any bonus upside that lasts longer.

# IT'S BETTER TO SELL EARLY AND BUY EARLY

The bulk of the timing of buying and selling activity is pretty predictable for all types of asset classes and investments, but almost everyone buys far later than they should. They also sell far later than they should.

It's pretty easy to argue that the intelligent investor is far better off, and is more successful, because they sell earlier and buy earlier. It is absolutely true that in some cases this may mean leaving a few dollars on the table. Far more importantly, though, you've avoided massive, deep, and devastating losses that would be many times the amount of any potential gains.

We as humans, even with the use of artificial intelligence, are terrible at pinpointing market timing, so it is wise to acknowledge and preempt this. Let your friends or salespeople laugh at you for your financial moves now. They won't be laughing later.

So many home sellers end up losing out on tens of thousands, hundreds of thousands, and sometimes millions of dollars. They overprice their homes when they hear the market is up. They pass on all the good offers. Then the market changes. If they are able to sell without losing it all (which many aren't), then they have to take deep losses. Then when it comes to buying houses, they typically wait until years into the recovery, when prices have often grown close to peaking again. They missed all the growth and end up in the same losing position again.

When is the best time to buy and sell?

The best time to buy is when there is maximum pessimism.

The best time to sell is when there is maximum optimism.

Otherwise, you are sure to miss out on double-digit figures.

Of course, if you plan to hold for the long term, through multiple cycles, then do not be scared into selling. The price you buy at now is highly likely to be far eclipsed after a couple more market cycles.

## Chapter 5

# TIMELESS PRINCIPLE #5: INVEST REGULARLY AND CONSISTENTLY

**Now that we've** covered the issues with volatility and market timing, this additional investment principle comes in as one of the core silver bullets for overcoming them. It brings together multiple principles, including the discipline to take action and to invest objectively.

We know that volatility is just a part of life and investing. It is a staple. We also know that at least up until now, neither humans nor our attempts at machine learning and AI are perfect at timing the market. Chess robots have been powerful for decades, but somehow, robo-advisors and traders just aren't nearly that effective for investing for the masses.

To succeed in investing, you have to be objective and take action — we've already covered some of the very costly risks of inaction and a lack of investing. We beat these issues and create profitable success habits by investing regularly and consistently.

# THE ADVANTAGES OF REGULAR AND CONSISTENT INVESTING

The commitment to investing regularly brings several advantages.

## Avoiding the Trap of Trying to Time the Market

When you focus on being consistent and investing all of the time, then you avoid all the unpleasantness and inefficiencies of trying to time the market, when you can't nail it perfectly anyway. You remove the fear and stress of trying to time the market, and the sleepless nights and distractions (like watching the ticker feed) that come with that. Not to mention the extremely expensive mistakes of poor timing decisions.

## Ensuring Your Money Is Always Being Put to Work for You

Committing to consistent investing means you aren't suffering the risks and costs of idle funds. You are religiously putting your money into play.

In turn, you won't be frozen by analysis paralysis.

## Creating a Positive Habit

All types of success are about positive habits. Some can seem very hard for some people to start, while bad habits seem to come very easily. But it doesn't take much to create a good habit. It just takes one small step at a time. It may even just be $100, or authorizing a future transfer. Those small, regular, and consistent steps and actions can turn into really big results, and what some see as "overnight" success.

Of course, once you start seeing the results, you get hooked. You never want to stop or take a break. The results keep on compounding, and not only make you feel good, but are healthy, too.

Running is a great example of this. When you start, or you've fallen into a long break, it can feel hard to begin. You may have to drag yourself out of bed. Start by walking a short distance. Then you can go bigger — walk farther, jog, then run. Once you are in the groove, you won't ever want to take a break from that routine.

## Changing Your Financial Dynamics

This process will help you with moving more and more of your income to being generated by your investments versus earned income.

A massive tax difference can exist between earned versus investment income. That's why people complain that the wealthy pay so much less in taxes than the middle class, despite earning far more each year.

Changing your financial dynamics ensures that you are consistently advancing toward financial freedom. If you already have it, this will continue to solidify your position and increase your disposable and investable income. If you aren't there yet, it will consistently reduce your risk and the impact of any stall or paring down of earned income, such as during crises or recessions, or due to health challenges.

# PUTTING IT INTO PLAY

Even with the best intentions, we are all super-busy today. Even though we know better, emotions can wreak havoc with our plans to be disciplined, too. It is understandable — but that doesn't mean you can use these factors as excuses. If you really want better for your life and those you care about, you have to find solutions. Fortunately, this doesn't have to be harrd.

## Dollar-Cost Averaging

Warren Buffett's mentor, Benjamin Graham, is credited with at least the term, if not concept, of intelligent investing using dollar-cost averaging.

Dollar-cost averaging means consistently investing at regular intervals without concern for pricing. Overall, the idea is that you will win, not only by leveraging the previously mentioned benefits of this principle, but because the price you buy in at and ultimate value you achieve will even out over time. The consistency will make up for any subpar pricing, as will being disciplined to invest at the perfect timing, even if you do it by accident.

This doesn't have to be the only investment tool and strategy in your quiver, but it should certainly be a part of your overall financial plan. (If you still feel like trying to time the market with some of your money, then this will at least offset some of the risk that you blow your timing.)

The idea is to treat investing like you buy groceries, not the rare occasion you may splurge on a diamond ring. You want healthy finances, so you should feed your investment portfolio consistently and regularly.

How often you choose to invest is up to you. It may also depend on how the rest of your finances are structured and when you receive income. This may be weekly, monthly, or quarterly — from a paycheck, annual bonus, investment returns, alimony payments, Social Security benefits, etc. You may make more sizable investments when you get your end-of-year bonus or at tax-refund time.

If your regular income seems to leave too little to make a meaningful investment or meet investment minimums on that schedule, then you can use a waterfall strategy. For example, if you can only afford to invest $1,000 per month, that can be set aside in a high-return savings account or added to your self-directed IRA or 401k throughout the year. Then you can roll that over annually into a superior investment in real estate, notes, or a fund.

## Automation

If you did have a grandmaster-beating chess robot that you could apply to manage your finances and investing, then it would certainly automate your investments. The more you automate, the more time you save, the more efficient and profitable your investing is, and the more disciplined you will be.

No matter what level you are at in your financial game, you can do a lot to automate this. You can use the waterfall strategy for consistently transferring and rolling over funds to invest.

(If you are happy with your current manager and fund, you can also instruct them to keep on reinvesting your profits and cash flow.)

## Chapter 6

# TIMELESS PRINCIPLE #6: INVESTING IS MOST INTELLIGENT WHEN MOST BUSINESSLIKE

**Most people do** not invest in a businesslike manner, which is of course why average, aka mediocre, results just aren't that appealing. Nor are they often worth the effort and sacrifice.

Why is investing better when it is "businesslike," and what does that even mean?

This means three things:

1. Invest objectively.
2. Be professional.
3. Be organized.

# INVEST OBJECTIVELY

Embracing our emotions can be a great thing in many areas of our lives. It's largely what makes life worth living. It just isn't a good investment strategy.

In fact, emotion is a downright horrific investment strategy; one that is almost certain to cost you a lot of money. It will surely make you break at least seven of the other investing principles in this book. That can't possibly lead to a good outcome, either financially or emotionally.

Most people still seem to approach investing, and especially real estate, as a hobby, an art, or a pastime. They buy the properties and construction materials that they like and would want for themselves. They base marketing, acquisition, and exit decisions on their personal tastes. Their emotions certainly drive their timing.

It doesn't take many of these emotional hobby sessions to mount up with some pretty hefty financial losses. It only takes one or two deadweight properties you can't get rid of to bankrupt most individual investors.

The home that you would choose to live in typically will not provide the best returns. The same applies to the finishings. In reality, the fact you love it may be what finishes you off — because you don't want to sell it when you should. You may not even want to lease it. You could just add another huge, bad debt in a house you will never use.

Emotions can especially wreak havoc with your direct investments in real estate. It may take a lot of self-control to deal with mortgage borrowers and tenants, especially when they blatantly take advantage of you, mess with your income and the value of your investments, or even maliciously try to victimize you. Still, you can't afford to mess up.

Someone wise once said that winning at investing isn't about beating anyone else, but "controlling yourself at your own game."

# BE PROFESSIONAL

The obvious meaning of this is: Carry yourself professionally. By all means, be yourself. Be authentic. Yet when dealing with others — from tenants to borrowers to financiers and Realtors — have some class. Being unprofessional or rude is bound to bite you back eventually. It can be costly.

This doesn't mean you are cold and heartless. You can be professional, demand the most from your customers and team, and still care. In fact, allowing the human element in, especially in how you treat your contractors, property managers, and other vendors, can make all the difference. It is rare in business today — which may be precisely why it can be so valuable.

The other part of being businesslike here is being business-minded. Detaching your emotions from the individual unit being traded is a big part of that. Don't think of an investment property as a house in your favorite vacation spot. It is just a number, and a unit to be held and traded.

This principle means that "business sense is knowing that the investment made will offer the investor the highest predictable annual compounding rate of return possible with the least amount of risk."

It means thinking like a responsible business owner. As a business owner, you certainly have responsibilities — legal and ethical ones. You are bound to do your best to get the most out of company capital and resources, and to be objective about making decisions that protect value and achieve growth. Even if you are only the CEO of your own finances and investment portfolio, viewing it this way can make a big difference in how you act and the results you achieve.

We've all seen the outcomes of the dangers of short-term thinking in business. It crushes even the biggest multi-billion-dollar organizations. Being professional means you not only want to see prompt results, but you are sure you are making the optimal choices for the long run, too.

# BE ORGANIZED

Successful businesses that survive and thrive are organized. Things run smoothly, they are more profitable, and they are less exposed to risk and the impacts of it. It is a lot more enjoyable for everyone in such businesses and everything they touch.

This applies just as much whether you are operating a real estate business or fund, or you are just managing your own personal finances and investment portfolio.

Having a plan is a good start to being organized. So is ensuring you have the right entities formed and in place. These may be an LLC, corporation, trust, or other tax-saving vehicle.

It means having thought about taxes and accounting, having well-orchestrated processes and systems, as well as removing bottlenecks so things can flow smoothly and efficiently, and you aren't held back when a great opportunity arises. It also means you aren't looking back and finding you left a whole lot of money on the table.

All the items in this section also happen to be pivotal when it comes to choosing others to work with in your investing.

## Chapter 7

# TIMELESS PRINCIPLE #7: IT'S NOT HOW MUCH YOU MAKE, BUT WHAT YOU GET TO KEEP THAT MATTERS

**One of the great** mistakes that new real estate investors and entrepreneurs make is confusing their top line and bottom line.

Ambition, constant growth, and thinking big can all be great, noble, and worthwhile pursuits. However, focusing solely on the top line and how much money you can flow through your hands in the short term can also be dangerously counterproductive.

New investors often get in, get hooked by how much they see they can make on their first deal or two, and then want to sprint and multiply that. The idea is to go fast and hit those milestones. Hit $1M a year, hit 10 deals a month, and on and on.

The problem is this often winds up leading to breaking the other timeless principles of investing, and ultimately the math and lifestyle aspirations just don't add up.

Despite the temporary media headlines that may suggest otherwise, a growth-at-all-costs, tunnel vision approach to the top line inevitably means problems. That's true of national economies, tech startups, and even companies momentarily valued at tens of billions of dollars, like Enron, Lehman Brothers, WeWork, and Zillow. It's rarely sustainable.

Let's take a look at both the dangers of ignoring the bottom line and the difference between the gross and net, plus how to optimize.

# THE GROSS PROBLEM

More gross money flowing through your accounts doesn't necessarily mean you are making more profit or spendable cash.

There can be advantages of size and economies of scale. Especially when it comes to access to bulk pools of distressed assets and mortgage notes. Yet investors need to do the full math and understand what is most important.

Multi-billion-dollar companies exist that lose billions of dollars each year. Those numbers may feed your ego, but not your bank account. Certainly, some entrepreneurs have built billion-dollar companies and then received zero when they had to sell their businesses. You have to decide which is most important to you.

The simplest way to put this principle is would you rather do 100 deals this year and only make a net profit of $2,000 on each, or do 10 deals and net $100,000 on each? That's an $800,000 difference in favor of doing fewer deals.

## The Dangers of a Gross-Only Focus

For a start, a gross-only focus probably means you are benching your more important goals, such as building wealth, generating usable income, and having more free time. It can take you in the opposite direction of those things.

That pressure to only hit the top line also brings many temptations. It can lead to rash mistakes. It has led many to try to take shortcuts or to abuse their most loyal partners and customers for temporary, short-term paper gains. Many have built very flawed structures in this process and have fallen into committing fraud. That always catches up with you.

## Where Most Blow it

Focusing on gross revenue or gross profit and punting worrying about the net down the road often puts real estate investors in the red. This is especially true when they get hit with big income tax bills by the IRS.

While TV "reality" shows have done a fantastic job at inspiring many to jump into flipping houses, they have also done a lot of financial damage. Their math is vague at best, and potentially a con. The numbers they pop up on the screen about how much they made on a flip at the end of an episode certainly don't show the net, or all of the costs. Most of those examples would actually be net losers at the end of the year.

Common areas that lead to losses between the gross and net include:

- Renovation cost and budget overruns
- Maintenance and replacements
- Property management
- Closing costs
- Time and labor

Risks are significantly heightened with tunnel vision on the gross, too. If you make only net $10,000 on a deal, and then find out you have to put in a brand-new HVAC system, you can be in the hole on that one item. If you had a $100,000 net projection, on the other hand, you can easily absorb several big surprise items and still make out with a nice net profit.

# UNDERSTANDING YOUR BOTTOM LINE

There are at least three critical elements to knowing and mastering your bottom line:

1. Your expenses
2. Risk-adjusted returns
3. Taxes

Make sure that you do all the math on your investments. Airbnb rentals are a great example of this. It sounds fantastic that you may lease them out for two to three times more gross per month than on an annual lease for the same unit — but your expenses may also be 50% higher.

The liability and risks of some investments are far higher, too. This is where risk-adjusted returns come into play. Understanding them will help you secure the best possible net profit.

Taxes are, of course, one of the largest parts of this and can make all the difference in your gross versus net and being net-profitable versus bankrupt. Taxes alone can make a double-digit difference in the net on each investment you make. In fact, when you compound that gain or loss each year over time, it will easily make a triple-digit difference in how much you have lost or gained. Debt service and operational efficiency can also make a substantial difference, but if there is one factor that is most pivotal, it is probably taxes.

# TACKLING TAXES FOR A BETTER BOTTOM LINE

One big difference between the most net successful and the rest is their attitude toward taxes.

Most people hide from taxes. They put their heads in the sand and hope taxes will go away, or at least kick the issue down the road until the last minute. If you do that, you will always pay a lot more in taxes.

Then there are the few (the wealthiest) who learned early to embrace taxes instead — to face them head on, and instead of only viewing them as a bill and expense, seeing them as a way to dramatically increase wealth, net returns, and cash flow.

Fortunately, many tools are available to legally minimize your tax liability and thus increase your net profitability. These include:

- Business entities like LLCs and S corps
- Self-directed IRAs and 401ks
- Multiple IRAs for the whole family
- 1031 exchanges
- Reinsurance
- Year-round tax plan for spending and investing
- Well-organized accounting records
- The best possible CPA and tax firm you can hire
- Trusts for minimizing taxes on succession plans

With these tools, you can maximize tax deductions, write-offs, and savings, while enjoying tax-deferred or tax-free returns that compound that way over time.

# TIME, LIFESTYLE, AND QUALITY OF LIFE

The benefits of sticking to this timeless principle of investing go well beyond the purely financial.

A blind focus on the gross typically means you are crazy-busy. You work far more hours and days for less profit. You have to do far more transactions. It is never enough. "Vacation" and "quality time" are not in your vocabulary. You have to do many more transactions to make the same amount of money. Not only are there far greater exposures to risks at that volume and pace, but the ROI on your time will be crushed.

Do the math and you might find that you are barely making minimum wage instead of making tens of thousands of dollars per hour.

If you watch the net, then no matter how many investments you make, the ROI on your time will be far, far higher. Scale based on that and you work toward your full potential.

With this mindset, you will have a lot more flexible time. You can choose to throw that into more real estate and investing as you choose. You also have the ability to enjoy your time doing other things. That may be just enjoying life, pursuing new adventures, working on self-growth, or being there for important moments for those you care about — birthdays, holidays, sports games, and crises. The benefits for your relationships will be enormous, just as the opposite will be true, too.

This is why some people seem to work so incredibly hard and are the most stressed out, with the least amount of time, while others are so much more successful and wealthier, and seem to have all the time in the world to enjoy life.

This principle and these factors are a large part of why I chose to offer fund investments to other investors — to help them boost their true net results, while maximizing their most important asset: their time.

## Chapter 8

# TIMELESS PRINCIPLE #8: UNDERSTAND WHAT YOU'RE INVESTING IN

**You can't expect** to make predictable returns and for your finances to go according to plan if you don't know what you are investing in.

Some have called this investing within your circle of competence.

There are two parts to this. The first is that if you don't understand what you are investing in, it is pretty difficult to know if you are making an intelligent investment. How do you know if it is a good deal, what you should pay for it, and if it has the foundations and mechanics needed to continue to fuel good performance?

The second part to this is the real definition of competence. It is not just about what you know now, but your ability to do something efficiently and successfully. Some things you can learn pretty easily, in which case, it may still be a good investment for you.

For example, maybe you have never painted a house or put down carpet before. Most people can learn how to do these things in a few minutes on YouTube to improve a house before flipping it.

Contrast this with biotech startups. If you don't know science, all the steps involved in passing regulatory approvals, the inner workings of venture capital firms that may come into play, or about hospitals who may be the company's customer, then that type of investment may be well outside your understanding or competence. It's probably not worth going to school for another seven years just to figure out whether this is a good investment or the business model and science are fatally flawed from the start.

You don't have to understand every detail and nuance. You do need to get the fundamentals.

# REAL ESTATE

Fortunately, real estate is one of those asset classes that everyone understands. At least to some extent.

Almost everyone has lived in a rental or owned a home or condo at some point in their lives. That's true whether it was with their parents who paid the rent or mortgage, student housing, moving in with roommates after school, or buying a home of their own.

Chances are high that you've encountered some of the basics of real estate. Maybe you've had to deal with applying for an apartment or mortgage, paying the rent each month, maintenance, or selling a home.

This all gives you some great insight into the experience, issues, and ways things work. You probably have some idea of what an outrageous amount of rent or house price is, or what just won't be appealing when it comes to renting or buying housing. This provides a great foundation for understanding common real estate investing strategies, like flipping houses, rentals, or mortgage lending.

Of course, you can expand into many other related areas as well, such as oil and gas, or timber and air rights — even real estate in China or Russia. Of course, this is where many get burned. They reach too far, and outside their circle of knowledge and competence. Remember the rules for investing for return of your capital first and for risk-adjusted returns.

# EASY-TO-TRACK BASICS AND TRENDS

An intelligent investment for the individual investor should offer easy-to-track basics and trends. Of course, deeper data and dynamics will exist that may not be accessible to the average amateur/outsider investor, but you should be able to get a good feel for the basics.

If you can go to the gym, local coffee shop, or diner and get a good sense for what others are buying and financing, or not, that's a strong start. It's pretty easy to tell if people are bullish on the market or tired of overpricing without having to rely on manipulated news headlines.

In real estate, there are some pretty obvious influencing factors, such as interest rates, how easily banks are approving mortgage loan applications, whether many rentals are available, or if lots of homes have For Sale signs in the yard.

It is often easy to spot shifting trends in real estate like this without waiting for the media to report what happened three months ago, once the data has been compiled and filtered.

This may be in stark difference to understanding other sectors, like cryptocurrency or publicly traded stocks in healthcare, technology, or manufacturing companies. If you know those industries intimately well, then by all means consider them for a portion of your overall investment portfolio. Just be aware that defaulting to putting money into them because everyone else is, without understanding them, is a surefire recipe for financial disaster.

# KNOWING WHO YOU'RE INVESTING WITH

When investing passively, such as through a partnership or fund, your priority is to understand who you are investing with.

This is far more important and efficient than the minutia of every individual unit being invested in. If your investment partners are buying and trading hundreds and thousands of investment units, you just can't evaluate each one in depth. It is not efficient or a good return on your own time.

Instead, you must pick a manager whom you respect and trust to do their job well, and whose investment philosophy, thesis, and criteria you understand. Do they have a strong track record? Are your values aligned? Do you understand why they are investing in what they are, and their plans for performance?

**Chapter 9**

# TIMELESS PRINCIPLE #9: KNOW THE PURPOSE OF EACH INVESTMENT

**Each investment you** make should have a specific purpose. It should work toward a specific goal, not just happen by default because you abdicated your financial decisions and were distracted by your day job. Don't fall into that trap.

Each investment you make, or each dollar you spend or use, for that matter, either takes you directly toward your goals or takes you away from them. You must know the purpose of each investment, as well as the costs when you aren't investing with focus and clarity.

# WHAT SHOULD YOUR NEXT INVESTMENT DO FOR YOU?

Exactly what the purpose of your next investment should be may depend on several factors. This includes what you have in your portfolio already, as well as your personal timeline and goals.

Some of these purposes may include:

- Future-proofing your finances
- Building finances for retirement
- Increasing your passive income
- Wealth preservation
- Wealth growth
- Specific purchase or spending goals
- Simplifying your investing
- Reducing exposure to tax liabilities

Of course, you may be saying to yourself that you want all these things. Real estate does have the unique power to simultaneously achieve multiple goals, although some asset types and strategies may be more geared toward some of these goals than others.

If you really have to have it all, then a hybrid fund that encompasses multiple investment strategies and asset types is probably for you.

# THE COST OF INVESTING WITHOUT FOCUS AND PURPOSE

One of the biggest cons in investing, finance, and work is fooling individual investors into default investing and abdicating their financial choices. It is often designed to sound confusing and hard, so you turn off and just let things happen. Not too different to politics and elections.

This enables many money and plan managers to invest and trade for their own interests and gains, not yours. It becomes about using your money to generate the highest commissions and fees for them.

That is true of your 401k, most pension funds, and brokerage accounts. Yet consider how much you make per hour at work versus the value of achieving your financial goals. Is it really intelligent to put in an extra hour of work versus taking an hour to make sure you are investing in alignment with your goals? Even if you make $300 or $500 an hour, that pales in comparison to hundreds of thousands — even millions — you could miss out on over the next two decades with mediocre, off-target investments. It is probably far less than the fees and commissions your broker will make on you in the next couple of years. The right investments can add double-digit compounding gains each year, even with the right tax strategy alone. Failing to think it through can cost you that much. Even if you are just starting out with $10,000 to invest, that can put you up or down by $2,000 in the next year.

What is the cost of falling short of your goals?

It probably includes taking on high-interest debt, paying more for everything, and experiencing lots of extra stress and disappointment.

You will look back on life with no time left to make up for those years and ask whether it was really worth it.

Not only will you certainly find that ignoring and shirking this investment principle has cost you millions of dollars in potential gains and income, but you will have lost the dreams of your lifestyle in retirement, your potential in life, and your ability to help others you love and to make a wider impact.

Ultimately, whether you invest directly for yourself or you use a fund manager, you should understand how each strategy and asset class works toward your goals rather than away from them.

## Chapter 10

# TIMELESS PRINCIPLE #10: FAILING TO PLAN IS PLANNING TO FAIL

**You may have** often heard that "Failing to plan is planning to fail" applies to business, but it equally applies to your finances, investing, and life itself.

If you don't have a plan (and a good, well-thought-out plan), then you are literally planning to fail. Many analogies for this exist, although it ultimately comes down to the fact that you probably have less than lottery-like odds of ending up where you really want to be without a compass and roadmap for where you want to go. If you haven't plugged the coordinates into the GPS or choose not to listen to it, then failing to arrive where you want to go and anywhere nearly on time is inevitable.

What are some of the key elements of an investment plan?

# CLARITY AND GOALS

A plan begins with clarity about your goals. What do you want the most? When do you want it? How much money and income will that take?

It is not just about the money, but money is the currency for affording most of most people's goals.

The best way to plan is to reverse-engineer it: Back out the math and moves you need to make to get where you want to go. For example, X in assets to achieve Y in income or returns will require Z to be invested.

# CREATING A SUSTAINABLE PLAN WITH LONGEVITY

This is where most investors completely blow it all.

It is far better to start with a 100-year plan and then to break that down to 20, 10, five, and one year. A few think about a five-year plan, but that typically ends up completely sabotaging what they really want for 10, 20, or 100 years out. Go long; break it down.

There is little benefit in creating seemingly huge success in the next one to five years if it means destroying your future and legacy after that. In fact, it will be quite painful.

This shows up in many ways in real estate investing.

One of the most common issues that catches real estate investors short is financing and over-leverage. Both of these are fantastic tools. Used well, they are some of the best advantages of investing in real estate. This doesn't mean that you have to personally take on a lot of debt or over-leverage. Other ways exist to achieve leverage, like partnerships, syndications, and funds.

One of the big newbie mistakes here is those who try to sprint and grow too fast, often using expensive, short-term debt for what should be long-term holds or faster flips.

It's that investor who takes a six- or 12-month loan, and then takes so long to finish the rehab and get the marketing and pricing right, they lose the property. Or those who try to upgrade to multi-family apartment complexes using five-year loans for something they want to hold for 20 or more years. There is no guarantee the capital markets and lenders will be there in five years, on what terms they will lend, or what that property will be worth. They may have gone from zero to 400 units in a year, although they might go from 400 to zero units much faster. Which, of course, isn't nearly as cool.

Other common pitfalls for newbies include shorting themselves on time-on-lease options, rent-to-own, and other creative financing structures. Then there is simply working on margins that are so thin they easily turn into negative cash flow.

Some models are just pyramid schemes, relying on the market staying the same or continuing to grow fast, often revealed when they grossly overpay for assets during upswings.

Even what should be experienced investors who have been in the industry for a decade can be caught off guard by rapidly rising inflation, and by failing to consider price in things like rising labor and material costs, property taxes, insurance, and more.

Then there is finding sustainability in strategy. Many real estate strategies can work during all phases of the cycle, but that doesn't necessarily mean they are the best main strategy all the time.

Fixing and flipping may be great, but there may be times when wholesaling makes more sense, or when flipping is more profitable than rentals or mortgage notes. Using all of them, and knowing when to shift more energy to one or the other, is an important part of sustaining for the long term, while minimizing losses or underperforming, and optimizing for the upside.

Management and customer service are also key to sustainability and longevity. They are often overlooked, or are where investors skimp to fatten up profit margins. Such short-term thinking will sink you. It can take years to build relationships, teams, trust, and customers who act as ambassadors. It only takes one shortsighted decision and email to burn it all.

As a real estate investor, you are in the customer service business. You can do a lot of good and have a great impact, while feeling great about your investments, if you do it with more care than the incumbent competition. If you follow bad examples when it comes to lending, servicing, leasing, and property management, don't expect your run in real estate to be sustained for long.

# PLANNING FOR MARKET CHANGES

As already touched on, part of smart planning is preparing for market changes — just like we prepare for volatility.

This includes not only strategies, but asset types as well. Consider commercial real estate and the industrial era. For a moment, company towns sprang up. There were fossil fuel mining towns, then towns built around physical office buildings. Some of these things are going extinct.

Then there are the inevitable ups and downs, when intelligent investors will see the moment to bulk up on capital to take advantage of coming acquisition opportunities. At other moments, it is raining gold out there and it pays to go flat out, scale, and take full advantage.

Truly intelligent investors will position themselves ahead of market changes, and transition for different stages of their finances and lives as well, perhaps moving from years of being an active investor to becoming a more passive investor, from focusing on wealth growth to preservation and income production.

# SUCCESSION PLANNING

Succession planning is one of the most significant parts of planning and shifts in life. Your entire life's work, investment decisions, sacrifice, and discipline in adhering to these principles can all come down to this.

It certainly isn't something that should be put off. We never know how much time we have. This is not only about the legal documents guiding your inheritance, but also about investing and putting your investments in the right vehicles to make the most of what you've built for your beneficiaries.

Even if it is not lost in transition, most wealth is rapidly wasted by the next generation — not intentionally, but because they don't know how to manage it.

Intelligent moves to beat these odds include:

- Having conversations about your investments and wishes early
- Sharing the principles in this book with your heirs

- Introducing heirs to your trusted advisors, money managers, CPAs, attorneys, etc.
- Using IRAs, trusts, and other entities to ensure swift, smooth, low-tax, low-cost transfers
- Having professional management and passive income-producing investments in place

# PLANNING FOR THE UNEXPECTED

When you think about it, not much should be truly unexpected. Not even natural or manufactured disasters, or global and national economic crashes. They are all a matter of when and how much, not if, and then how you will mitigate that risk, or come out a winner.

Never say "never." Anything can happen. Anything that can happen will at some point. With this in mind, it is wise to plan for so-called unexpected or rare events, as well as the things we don't think will change — like flying cars and drone delivery, space tourism, or that fabled California mega-earthquake.

Nothing is a problem if you plan for it, and choose to find a way to come out on top.

# TAXES

We've already covered some of the importance of taxes when it comes to net gains and what you get to keep. Taxes should only be cringeworthy when you have slacked on your planning.

Together with your tax experts and personalized advice, you can turn this into an area of advantage, even enabling you to offer more for properties than your competitors and undercutting them in other areas, while still netting more.

You should have a tax plan throughout the year for maximizing savings, as well as for the long term and your passing.

# PLANNING YOUR INVESTMENT CONTRIBUTIONS

An important part of planning is planning your investment contributions.

How often will you roll money over into investments? How much will you invest each year?

Several factors can influence your choices here:

- Current annual contribution limits to various tax-saving vehicles, like IRAs
- Your personal time frame for achieving your goals
- The percentage of your income that you can dedicate to saving and investing

One of the most important factors here is, of course, time. The earlier you start saving and investing, the lower the percentage of your income that you will need to set aside to reach your goals.

According to Ally, if you started saving 10% of your income at age 25, you'd have double as much by the time you hit 65 as if you only started investing at 35 years old, and around four times as much as if you waited until you were 45 years old. If you put aside 15% of your income starting at 25, you'd have around five times as much as if you began at 45.

Put another way, if you put off investing until you are 45, you may have to carve out 40% of your income to hit the same result as if you put away just 10% starting at 25. That's a big difference.

If you begin investing a higher percentage of your income earlier in life, you may not need to save any of your income in your later working years.

# DON'T GET BOGGED DOWN IN PLANNING

Planning is important. It is vital. Just don't let it get in your way of taking action and producing results.

Having an annual and multi-year plan is much more efficient. You've already decided what to do. You don't have to debate it and redo all the math every month or quarter. However, you don't want to spend months trying to craft the perfect financial plan, only to discover so much is going to change anyway while you've missed out on some of the best investment opportunities of your life.

Some years, you won't make as much as you hoped. In other years, you may have big expenses you didn't plan on. Some years will be home runs that mean you have a lot more to invest and need more tax breaks.

Remember, many things will change, from tax rates to contribution limits to retirement accounts, and more.

Create a simple, actionable financial plan and goals. Be flexible in how you achieve them. Revisit the plan briefly every year to tweak it as needed or desired.

## Chapter 11

# TIMELESS PRINCIPLE #11: LOCATION, LOCATION, LOCATION

**One of the** most common sayings you'll hear about success in real estate is that it is all about "location, location, location."

There is certainly some truth in this. Yet many get it horribly wrong, and grossly misunderstand what it really means.

Location is important. Some locations are far more valuable than others. Some offer far more growth and safety than others. However, to make this principle work for you, I believe it is wise to zoom out and gain a fuller perspective across time and the map.

## PRIME, ULTRA-PRIME, AND TIME

One of the big mistakes that investors make with location is assuming that the most prime or "ultra-prime" locations of the moment are the best investments. Some of them may have been considered prime for decades. That can fool your mind into believing they will always be that way.

Silicon Valley, California, is a great example of this. It has only really been popular, or an economic hub, for around 40 years. If you were born in the 1960s, it may have seemed like prime real estate your whole adult life, but it wasn't like that before the 1980s. It was a few people working on projects and tinkering with inventions in their garages, and farmland. MAore recently, you may have noticed many companies moving away from there again.

New York City may have a longer history as a financial hub. Yet it has had an ongoing battle, often losing its ranking as the financial capital of the world to cities in Europe and even Asia. When you are reading this, Manhattan may or may not be an attractive place to live. The shift away from the industrial era, when offices and high-street shopping were important pillars of location, may have certainly changed the definition of prime, too.

What about coastal areas and vacation hot spots? What about highly craved waterfront real estate? Extremely high premiums have been put on condos with ocean views, or houses on the front line of the beach. That's fantastic if you have one for yourself to live and vacation in. Yet aside from the increased risks of these locations due to weather or building on sand, not even the coast and view will stay the same forever.

While some locations may be able to afford to continue to replace the sand and coastline, no matter what the cost, not all will. Most of these remedial activities don't last long at all. That means that what might have been waterfront 100 years ago is underwater today. Those cheaper properties a couple of miles back may now be the waterfront. This will obviously substantially change values and actual locations.

This is not about debating climate change. There are places around the world and in the United States where you can see these changes for yourself.

Views, of course, also fluctuate. Unless you own all the building rights and air rights around you, a new, taller building can easily pop up in a year, wiping out that pricey view you paid the premium for.

# WHAT'S TRENDING: LOCATION VS. RETURNS

Another major blunder that not only investors, but many home buyers routinely make is buying into trends. They think a smart location and investment is about what fashionable neighborhood is being advertised in magazines this month.

What's in fashion never stays the same. It might be cyclical, but it is not static. If you have teenagers, you've probably laughed at how they think they invented skinny jeans and never thought that would change. Then flares came back. The same is true of real estate.

The hip, gentrifying, or luxurious neighborhood of this month probably wasn't so cool or pricey two years ago. It probably won't be so trendy 10 or 20 years from now. Now if you are flipping real estate in 30 days or less, these can be great locations to cash in on — just not so great if you are buying your lifetime dream home, or maybe a rental to hold for 100 years. These probably are peaking right now.

Look at Brooklyn, New York. For a long time, it was the armpit of New York City. Then it became hip. Prices rocketed. It even surpassed

Manhattan in prices and coolness for a while. Then, of course, it became mainstream.

These same trends have played out everywhere, with great examples in South Florida, California, Washington state, and Texas.

In this respect, the best location to invest in can depend on your investment strategy and timeline, especially how long you will hold it. Today's B and C class neighborhoods often become the hot places to be a couple of years from now. That means they will probably offer the most growth in prices and rents at that time.

If you are looking for low-risk, wealth-preservation, and ready-to-go investments, one location might be right for you. If you are prepared to renovate, take your time to build up property performance, and can deal with more intensive property management, you may find far higher returns somewhere else.

# THE FUNDAMENTALS

Experienced investors who constantly evaluate the map for the best places to invest home in on the fundamentals. Three of the enduring fundamentals that are unlikely to ever become irrelevant are:

1. Affordability
2. Investor-friendliness
3. Crime

If you can only choose one factor to evaluate a destination, it should probably be affordability. Affordability alone is the best indicator of where you are in the real estate cycle, potential for growth, longevity of returns, as well as value.

One quick hack here is to gauge affordability of rents and properties to buy against what the most likely end retail users of those properties can afford. Once pricing reaches levels that can only be afforded by speculative investors and flippers tossing the hot potato, you've probably reached the peak.

Investor-friendliness is very important. An anti-investor climate is likely to continue to make things more difficult for you, while eroding value, cash flow, and returns. Issues include ever-increasing taxes, harsher rent controls, eviction bans, high fines, and laws and courtrooms that heavily favor tenants over landlords.

Crime rates are highly influential as well. High crime rates lead to businesses moving out, investment leaving, declining aesthetics, reduced demand, lower rents, and decreasing prices. Rising crime rates create a downward spiral. However, the opposite is true, too.

Perhaps no less important, but secondary to these factors, is a location's ability and track record in innovating and reinventing itself. This differentiates those boom/bust mining-like towns that fade and turn into ghost towns and ruins from those that are able to bounce back and keep growing over time.

Some places just seem able to keep on doing this. They have that entrepreneurial spirit and refuse to be kept down. Some great cases of this occurred in the Midwest with places that reinvented themselves as healthcare centers or other hubs after the auto industry collapsed. In the South, small and sizable towns have seized on high-speed internet and offered financial incentives to lure top talent, businesses, and investment to help them modernize. Some do this with tourism. If a location can keep on updating like this, it will find a way to keep thriving, even after a big crash.

Then there are some exceptions to these factors, and fundamentals that can change and become less influential over time. Great examples of these were schools, job numbers, sizable local employers, and diversification of industry.

It used to be that local employment rates, the presence of large employers, and a base of diverse employers were key to the fundamentals of a location. There have always been exceptions to this, such as Key West, Florida — a vacation destination, where property prices had little to do with what locals could afford versus what international investors could splurge on for vacation homes in their favorite destination and for tax and legal shelters. Of course, rents there are also largely based upon tourism.

Now that most people may not live within 1,000 miles of their employers and we may have surpassed the tipping point for virtual learning instead of physical classrooms, those may no longer be check marks on your list of criteria when evaluating a location. People can now earn Manhattan and Silicon Valley or overseas wages, yet live in a small town in Alabama where property taxes are very low and they get a lot more house for their money.

It's never about whether somewhere is a "good" or "bad" location. Rather, it is about whether a location best matches your personal goals, investment strategy, and timeline.

## Chapter 12

# TIMELESS PRINCIPLE #12: DON'T BLINDLY FOLLOW THE HERD

*"When everyone is going right, look left."*— *Sam Zell*

**This principle supports** many of the other principles in this book. Winning at being objective, profiting from volatility, avoiding losing money, and staying consistent are all intertwined with this principle of not blindly following the herd.

## RUNNING WITH THE HERD

Running with the herd isn't always a terrible thing. A herd can provide some level of safety. Being toward the front means you are less likely to get picked off by the wolves at the back. You may even be able to steer the herd yourself.

In some real estate investment scenarios, being among the herd can actually be beneficial in supporting your strategy — for example, house-flipping and new construction. When everyone is bullish on the market and paying premium prices, and being swept away by emotion as new construction developments sell out in minutes to lines of buyers camped out overnight, it can be a great time to fix and flip, or build. There are gains that you may not want to miss out on.

This makes the "blindly" part of this principle a very important part of it. The herd is an indicator, and it can be leveraged to your advantage. Just understand how you want to be different from them. You want to be aware, not trampled in the stampede or carried over the side of a cliff or into the lion's mouth because you are following everyone else.

# CONTRARIAN INVESTING

Going the opposite way of the herd, or contrarian investing, is where the most wealth has been made. It is certainly where the most retained leaps in wealth have been made.

Going with the herd can help fill your buckets when it is raining gold. Yet as people continue to follow the herd, those easy gains are typically lost just as quickly.

Again, this is not just being contrarian for the sake of it. Be aware and intentional, and think for yourself. Watching the herd can certainly be a leading indicator of where you don't want to go.

Sam Zell is probably one of the most famous contrarian investors — a multi-billionaire real estate investor who famously made most of his wealth buying up distressed properties for pennies on the dollar, and then flipping many of his assets to big funds like Blackstone for tens of billions of dollars, just before they plummeted in value and ended up underwater.

This is, again, about the discipline to sell when the market is up and at its most optimistic, and having the guts to buy when the market is crushed and everyone seems fearful. You might seem crazy to sell or buy at these moments, although, in hindsight, it always seems obvious that it was the right move.

I probably took my first real dive into contrarian investing in the 2007 Great Recession. I did that by buying nonperforming mortgage loan notes at a time when most people probably thought it was insane. Property prices were down, and the big banks hadn't managed to collect on these loans. My fund was able to buy them up at 60% discounts or even better. With the right approach to management, they ended up being worth a whole lot more. When others saw that, they wanted to invest millions of dollars along with my partner and me to benefit from what we were doing.

# INTELLIGENT AND EFFICIENT CONTRARIAN INVESTING

While the wisdom in contrarian investing is obvious, it is the execution that often scares investors and keeps them frozen in the status quo, to their eventual demise.

Those who haven't been diversified in their investment strategies may find it daunting to completely change the only thing they know how to do, even if that means continuing to flog the dead horse for far too long. Pivoting their strategy may require upgrading their knowledge, learning a whole new business, building a new network, and starting almost from scratch, only to have to do that all over again for the next shift. Not everyone wants this to be their full-time career. Even those who do can be resistant to change.

There also can be the high transactional costs of liquidating an entire portfolio and reinvesting it. And again, and again.

I've found the optimal method for easily moving around the herd without big-strategy learning curves, infrastructure adjustments, or high-volume transactional costs is through a hybrid fund — one that already encompasses a wide variety of investment strategies and asset classes. The fund itself will adjust and weight itself in these strategies and assets appropriately, and stay slightly ahead of the herd. They deal with all the transitions and transactions. As an investor in a fund like this, you simply collect your same ongoing dividends.

## Chapter 13

# TIMELESS PRINCIPLE #13: FORTUNE FAVORS THOSE WHO TAKE ACTION

*"The future depends on what you do today."*— *Gandhi*

**They say "fortune favors the bold"** Pablo Picasso said, "Action is the foundational key to all success." Tony Robbins puts it as, "The path to success is to take massive, determined actions."

It's all about action.

Whether you are concerned about what your money is invested in right now, know you need to start investing in real estate, or have finally had enough of not achieving the results you really want and are capable of, the only thing standing between you and where you want to be is action.

No matter where you are on your own financial journey, this book should have reminded you of some vital lessons, given you new food for thought, and provided new insights to work with. Yet none of it will produce any value unless you put it into use and take action on it.

# WHEN IS THE IDEAL TIME TO TAKE ACTION?

Most people get stuck between thinking it is too late or thinking they need to wait.

Of course, if you wait, you will probably start thinking you are too late.

The best time to start taking new action may have been yesterday, but there will be no better time to start than today. This is true no matter what your financial situation is, and regardless of where you think the market is. There may never be a "perfect" time, except for right now.

# PROPELLING ACTION

If you sometimes struggle to take action as swiftly as you should, there are ways to help propel yourself to do it.

## Penalties vs. Rewards

Everyone is motivated a little differently. It is in our DNA to avoid pain and gravitate toward pleasure, yet some of us respond more to the threat of punishment, while others are more motivated by attaining rewards. Set up a system for yourself to motivate your action based on this.

You could penalize yourself for failing to take action, such as forgoing eating out until you've restructured your portfolio or made your next investment. If you keep procrastinating, you may up the ante. Maybe you'll be as bold as vowing to sell the dream car you just bought unless you rectify your financial situation, or canceling the vacation you just booked for yourself.

If you find rewards more compelling, then set some up for yourself. That may be enjoying the largest size of your favorite coffee once you've completed your new financial plan. It could be eating out with the family at your favorite restaurant to celebrate closing your next big investment. Or booking that big dream vacation for next year as a reward for the investments you are making, and what they are going to do for you.

Accountability partners are also a fabulous resource. They'll keep you going and making progress, even when you feel like slacking off. This may be a professional mastermind group or family and friends. Let them know your big plans, make big claims, and they'll help you figure out how to do it. If you don't take that action, they'll be prompting you for updates.

# WHERE TO START TAKING ACTION

The best place to start is with a simple one- to three-step action plan. Start crossing off those steps, then add one or two more top to-dos as you make progress.

The simpler, cleaner, and more actionable this to-do list, the more likely you will follow through.

## The quick three-step action plan

1. Write out your top three financial goals.
2. Pick one new type of investment to get you to those goals.
3. Fund that investment.

# Conclusion

There you have it: 13 of the most important, timeless principles for investing in real estate. In fact, if you dug into and carefully read each section, you probably extracted additional principles you will want to apply to your own finances and real estate investing.

There may be moments when you are tempted to diverge from these principles. Or maybe you will find an excuse in a moment that sounds like it justifies breaking one of them. It is almost certain you will regret that sooner or later.

These principles are here to guide you to your increasing and lasting success — to help you get from here to there, enjoy even greater results than you thought possible, and keep the gains you make. Don't think of them as rules that box you in or tell you what to do, but rather as wise, friendly guides to accompany you on your journey to empower you to win.

I've specifically selected those for this book that have worked for thousands of years and that appear they will never devalue.

# MAKING THE MOST OF THESE PRINCIPLES

Knowledge alone won't protect you or fuel your wins. You have to put these principles to use.

Just like it doesn't matter that you know an incredibly wise yogi or monk if you can't reach them for help because they are off hiding in a cave meditating for the next nine years, you need to keep these allies close. As you would your GPS, or a best friend whom you know you can call up any time of day or night.

One great way to do this is to print out these principles as a list or turn them into a graphic. Keep them posted prominently at your work space, or by your bed, so you can review them along with your goals first thing every morning and last thing at night.

If you want to be more environmentally friendly and ensure they are always with you, then you can save them as the screen saver on your laptop or phone. This way, they can act as a daily decision guide. You might be surprised at how often they can instantly aid you in making a quick decision about a deal you have been debating. You'll be able to sleep much better knowing that you are making the right decision, and be able to jump out of bed in the morning with clarity for the day ahead.

## The Timeless Principles of Investing in Real Estate

1. Diversify, Diversify, Diversify
2. Don't Lose Money
3. Expect Volatility and Profit from it
4. Don't Be Fooled into Thinking You Can Time the Market Perfectly
5. Invest Regularly and Consistently
6. Investing Is Most Intelligent When Most Businesslike
7. It's Not How Much You Make, But What You Get to Keep that Matters
8. Understand What You're Investing in

9. Know the Purpose of Each Investment

10. Failing to Plan Is Planning to Fail

11. Location, Location, Location

12. Don't Blindly Follow the Herd

13. Fortune Favors Those Who Take Action

# LEARN AND SHARE

If you want to learn more about how other successful people and organizations are applying these principles, I encourage you to tune into the Passion for Real Estate Investments podcast (PFREI).

The NNG Capital Fund blog also publishes weekly insights on the market, how to leverage various strategies, and how principles like these are relevant to what you are experiencing out there.

You can also connect with us on your favorite social media networks to see how your peers are engaging the market with these principles, and to share any that you believe I've missed, as well as ask any questions you have about their application or to show others how they are working for you.

There is plenty of opportunity for all of us to succeed together. While you can do it on your own, the journey is certainly better enjoyed when we go on this venture together.

# About the Author

**Investor, wealth manager,** educator, and proud father of two incredibly financially savvy sons, Fuquan Bilal has spent more than 21 years operating businesses and perfecting his proprietary formulas for investing in real estate and other alternative asset classes.

When he's not in the office, you might catch Fuquan running to the gym, experimenting with new tweaks to his personal performance, taking on new challenges, exploring new markets with his kids, or hosting the Passion for Real Estate Investments (PFREI) podcast.

As the founder and chief visionary officer of NNG Capital Fund, Fuquan has proven to deliver to investors through a variety of funds over the years, most notably when it comes to providing attractive risk-adjusted returns and achieving predictable levels of passive income.

He is one of the few leaders in this arena who has proven to come through and level up through periods of national and global economic distress and prosperity.

What may really separate Fuquan from others, in addition to his magnetic personality, is the care he has for sustainably managing his clients' funds, as well as managing his teams and treating them well, and caring about the communities where his firms operate.

While these may seem fluffy to some, they are absolutely the differentiator when it comes to survival and the ability to thrive for companies, funds, and reputations, and all of those counting on them.

If you haven't yet, be sure to catch up on Fuquan's first three books (available on Amazon): Turning Distress into Success, about how to navigate tough markets; The Tire Kicker, about taking action; and The Guide to Diversifying in Real Estate for the Intelligent Real Estate Investor.

# About NNG

**NNG Capital Fund** is an alternative investment firm specializing in real estate assets and mortgage debt investments for passive investors. Originally born as a solution for the inefficiencies that Fuquan Bilal experienced in the investment arena and to invest his own capital more wisely and profitably, NNG's series of funds have proven incredibly popular with other sophisticated investors as well.

NNG Capital offers access to superior investments with industry-leading performance, accountability, and transparency. The firm is built on these timeless investment principles, while consistently embracing innovation and constantly striving for greater results. It is built on shared successes, intelligent investing, and an openness to finding better ways to do things. It's about investing safely and more profitably, while treating everyone the company touches the way they ought to be.

## Future-Proofing Your Investment Portfolio

NNG Capital is the pioneer of the hybrid fund — an investment fund that empowers individuals and other firms to invest well, with a solidly formulated diversified portfolio, for simplified investing, passive income, and winning both the short and long game. It is perhaps the first fund that enables investors to maximize their upside while adhering to these timeless investment principles.

Be sure to subscribe to the NNG blog and connect with NNG on your favorite social networks to keep track of the latest developments and performance.

www.ingramcontent.com/pod-product-compliance
Lightning Source LLC
Chambersburg PA
CBHW071438210326
41597CB00020B/3842